ALAN RANGER

Krupp Protze Lorry

STRATUS

Published in Poland in 2020
by Wydawnictwo Stratus sp.j.
Po. Box 123,
27-600 Sandomierz 1, Poland
e-mail: office@wydawnictwostratus.pl

as
MMPBooks
e-mail: office@mmpbooks.biz

www.mmpbooks.biz
www.wydawnictwostratus.pl

ISBN: 978-83-65958-79-2

Editor in chief
Roger Wallsgrove

Editorial Team
Bartłomiej Belcarz
Robert Pęczkowski
Artur Juszczak

Cover concept
Dariusz Grzywacz

Book layout concept
Dariusz Grzywacz

All photos: author's collection except stated

DTP
Wydawnictwo Stratus sp.j.

PRINTED IN POLAND

Foreword

In this series of books, I have no intention of trying to add to what is already a very well documented history of Germany's Krupp Protze 6-wheel off road light truck as it has been covered by many previous publications, notably *Tank Power Vol. CXC Number 454* by Janusz Ledwoch. Here I hope to give an impression, through original photographs from my collection taken both during and before war, of the various versions of the Krupp Protze 6-wheelers and their crews as they dealt with the conditions and circumstances in which they found themselves, in all the theatres of operations in which they served.

In this publication I hope to show what was seen through the lens of the normal German soldier's camera, the soldiers that had to live with and operate these vehicles each and every day, not the professional PK cameramen whose well posed and sanitized shots are well known and have been published over and over again. As such, they have already been seen by most interested parties. However, the images taken by individual soldiers show a more personal view of the vehicles in which the soldiers both lived and worked, the views that interested the common soldier rather than the professional propagandist. For the most part these photographs have been in private collections and have only recently come onto the market.

Most images we have used here were taken from prints made on old German Agfa paper stock and the majority of these original prints are no more than 25 mm by 45 mm in size. Whilst we have used the best quality photos from my collection, occasionally, due to the interesting or the rare nature of the subject matter, a photo of a lesser quality has been included.

Introduction History

After the First World War Germany was plunged in to a great depression and this had a marked effect on new vehicle design and production. Basically, design stagnated as development costs were just too expensive. However, by the mid 1920s, Germany's industrial base was beginning to look forward to a brighter future and development of new vehicles and other equipment restarted, albeit at a very slow pace. Initially Krupp had been manufacturing an off-road 3 ton truck focused on the agricultural market and regions without a modern road network. This truck, the Krupp L 2 H 163, was a 6-wheel vehicle with 4-wheel drive (6x4) and with a few minor militarization modifications had also been sold to the German *Reichswehr* (the German Army prior to 1935). Krupp identified as early as 1929 that a lighter variant of this heavy truck design might have a better commercial future, so began the design of a light 6x4 truck under their own initiative. The vehicle was to be based on a ladder frame chassis with the motor mounted in the front, with front wheel steering and twin driven rear axles. Krupp gave the vehicle the designation of L 2 H 43. The prototype of this new vehicle was ready for testing by 1932. It differed from all subsequent versions by having a normal style truck bonnet/engine cowl, as originally the design called for the chassis to be fitted with a diesel engine. However it was decided during development that, to keep costs as low as possible, Krupp would install one of their own air-cooled 4-cylinder horizontally opposed petrol engines, so from vehicle No. 2 onwards the familiar slopped bonnet that became the defining feature of the type was installed. An air-cooled engine, not needing a fluid cooling radiator or its large grill, and a lower profile "boxer" layout, led to the sloping bonnet with its domed starter cover that covered the starter handle's dog clutch. A flat engine, also known as a horizontally opposed engine, is a piston engine where the cylinders are located on either side of a central crankshaft. The most common configuration of flat engines is the 'boxer engine', where each pair of opposed cylinders moves inwards and outwards at the same time. This gave rise to the troop's unofficial nickname for the type, "The Krupp Boxer". After the production of twenty prototypes and significant testing during 1933, the L 2 H 43 entered series production in 1934.

With the Nazis taking control of Germany in 1933, the whole future of this new truck changed from being a private development by Krupp that held inherent risk as to its success, to a certain winner. The new German government poured funds into expanding the German military with a priority towards its motorization, and the new Krupp light 6x4 off road truck was in demand as both a troop carrier and a light prime mover from the very start. Indeed its production became exclusively for the military, without a single unit being sold to a civilian customer despite its original design criteria.

The Krupp L 2 H 43 was powered by the Krupp flat-4 air-cooled engine type M-302 that produced 50 hp and gave the vehicle a top road speed of 65 kph, with an off-road top speed of 25 kph. It was fitted with two fuel tanks that stored a total of 70 litres (42+28) giving it a maximum range of 150 km off-road and 270 km on a good road surface.

Following reports back from units in service in the field, the vehicle's chassis was improved to give a larger clearance between the two rear axles to reduce fouling. The chassis frame was widened by 40 mm from 860 mm to 900 mm, and the M-302 engine was dropped in favour of the new improved version with the designation Krupp type M-304. It had slightly improved power of 55 hp that gave the vehicle a top road speed of 70 kph with an off-road top speed of just over 25 kph. Krupp also simplified the front mudguards and fitted a full width front bumper. All these changes culminated with the vehicle being given a new designation by Krupp, type L 2 H 143, and this new improved version replaced the old L 2 H 43 in production from February 1937 onwards until production of the Krupp Protze was terminated in 1942.

By far the majority of the Krupp Protze production was delivered in two versions, the *Protzkraftwagen* Kfz. 69 *mit Fahrgestell des I.gILkw*, (Kfz. 69) and the *Mannschaftkraftwagen* Kfz. 70 *mit Fahrgestell des I.gILkw*, (Kfz. 70).

The **Kfz. 69** was built as a light prime mover for either the 37 mm Pak36/37 German anti-tank gun or the light infantry howitzer the 75 mm leIG 18/40, with ammunition stowage down each side of the rear cargo area, with seating in the middle for four crew and a bench seat up front in the cab for the driver and one other.

The **Kfz. 70** was built as a light troop carrier with an open topped wooden rear cargo area with bench style seats running front to back down both sides providing seating for up to 10 fully equipped infantrymen and a bench seat up front in the cab for the driver and one other.

The Krupp Protze was built in other variants as well, but not in anywhere near the same numbers as the two mentioned above. Amongst these variants were the following:

Kfz. 19 *Fernsprechbetriebskraftwagen mit Fahrgestell des I.gILkw.*
  (Field Telephone exchange van built on the I.gILkw chassis)
  It had a wooden van-style enclosed body for a crew of 5.

Kfz. 19 (Late) *Funkkraftwagen*
  (Radio Communications Vehicle)
  A radio signal booster vehicle with a wooden van-style enclosed body that had the "Maratze" antenna
    mounted on the roof. (the "Maratze" was a large bed frame style aerial made from steel tubing).

Kfz. 21
  This was to be a senior staff car variant but the type never entered production. Two very different prototypes
  are known to have been completed at least, one with a coachwork built body with a plush interior for very
  high ranking officers that was put on show at the Wien motor show of March 1941. A simplified sheet steel
  bodied staff car prototype was also manufactured, that was able to seat up to 4 officers in the back and with
  2 crew seats in front.

Kfz. 61 *Funkkraftwagen*
  (Radio Communications Vehicle)
  This was a radio operators truck fitted with a wooden van-style enclosed body.

Kfz. 68 *Funkmastkraftwagen*
  (Radio Aerial Mast Vehicle)
  This vehicle had a fully enclosed wooden van-style body with a 15 meter (when extended) telescopic aerial
  mounted on the rear body panel when is use and stowed on the roof during transit. However this vehicle
  once in service proved to have an internal working area that was much too small for its intended role and so
  it was cancelled. This function was then carried out by various 3 ton trucks fitted with a similar but much
  larger crew compartment, consequently this variant of the Krupp was very rare.

Kfz. 83 *Leichter Scheinwerferkraftwagen I.*
  (60 cm Searchlight Prime Mover, Type 1)
  This vehicle was fitted with a custom-built open rear body that included a petrol-fuelled electrical generator
  to power the 60 cm towed searchlight and was also fitted with seating for a crew of four plus a driver.

Kfz. 83 *Leichter Scheinwerferkraftwagen II.*
  (60 cm Searchlight Prime Mover, Type 2)
  This vehicle was fitted with a custom-built open rear body fitted with a spares locker for the 60 cm searchlight that replaced the electrical generator of the earlier variant and was also fitted with seating for a crew
  of five plus a driver.

Krupp manufactured over 7,000 of the L 2 H 43 and L 2 H 143 combined, from this total three L 2 H 143s were exported to Poland in 1938 from an order for 50 but this order was destined not to be fulfilled due to Germany's invasion of Poland in 1939. Another 627 L 2 H 143s were exported to Hungary between 1937 and 1939.

Three further L 2 H 143 chassis were issued to Dak en Werf Maalschappij Wilton-Fijenoord in occupied Holland who mounted a primitive armoured body on it producing an armoured car with a rotating turret. The vehicle was armed with two machine guns, one in the forward lower hull and one in the turret. One of these odd-looking vehicles survived the war and was to be found parked in the courtyard of the Neue Reichskanzlei in Berlin, where it had belonged to the *Verstarker* Police Unit. Ten of the L 2 H 143 chassis were also used as the base of the first production batch of the Sd.Kfz. 247 Ausf A armoured artillery observation and command vehicles, the later Ausf B variant being based on Horch's 4-wheel armoured car chassis. Krupp had developed and produced prototypes of a successor to the L 2 H 143, the L 2 H 243. It was essentially a beefed-up version of the same vehicle that was fitted with drive to all six wheels and a 70 hp V8 petrol engine. However this development was brought to an abrupt halt as it was not included in the list of preferred vehicles that were to be included in the German government's production rationalization program titled the "Schell Programme". The L 2 H 243's intended role was mostly taken up by variants of the Mercedes and Steyr 1500 series of 4-wheel drive vehicles.

Lastly of note is that a considerable numbers of the Krupp Protze trucks were converted by their crews and or field maintenance units as the war progressed, into weapons carriers armed with either the 37 mm Pak 36/37

Anti-tank gun or a 20 mm Flak gun. Photographic evidence shows that both the 20 mm Flak 30 and Flak 38 were mounted in these weapons carrier conversions and I have also seen one photo of a Krupp Protze weapons carrier conversion mounting a 50 mm Pak 38 anti-tank gun. This was probably a one-off conversion as this gun's weight and recoil forces would have severely overstretched the Krupp's chassis capabilities.

Overall the Krupp Protze was well liked by its crews, its ease of maintenance and reliability and good cross-country performance compared to other vehicles of its day made it stand out as a success. However its relatively low-powered engine that restricted its towing capacity eventually rendered it obsolete, as bigger and heaver weapons systems became the norm and simpler, and indeed cheaper, vehicle designs entered the fray in the late 1930s. But considering that the Krupp Protze was designed a full ten years before the war, its qualities ensured that it stands out as a design classic to this day.

This Krupp Protze L 2 H 43. Kfz.70 is seen driving in a field alongside the main road whilst the rail crossing just in the background is under repair, in March of 1941 in northern Belgium just outside the town of Aalst. The soldier in the foreground in front of the truck is removing an obstacle that is blocking the Krupp's path through the mud.

Krupp Protze L 2 H 43

A Krupp Protze L 2 H 43. Kfz. 69 belonging to a towed Anti-Tank Gun Company, as denoted by the tactical symbol on the front left mudguard, has been photographed here in the high summer of 1941 driving along a dirt track in Norway, followed by a motorcycle and sidecar and another Krupp behind that.

Here a motorized Anti-Tank Gun unit is seen parked up in the gardens of a Warsaw suburb waiting for the order to move off on the day's march. We can see here in the foreground an Sd.Kfz. 10 1 ton half-track with three Krupp Kfz. 69s alongside it. Outside the garden fence we see more Sd.Kfz. 10s.

A very nice close-up of a German Army mechanic working on the steering linkage of a Krupp L 2 H 43. The view gives us a very good look at the front suspension and bumper mounted number plate, as well as the vehicle's iconic starter dog cover.

This is a typical early war picture of a motorized Anti-Tank unit, this one seen in northern France in the summer of 1940. With the lack of suitable motorized transport the Pak 37/37 37mm anti-tank guns are towed by Krupp Kfz. 69s, but the remainder of the gun crews that can't fit on the Kfz. 69 trucks are equipped with BMW R12 motorcycles with side cars, instead of the Krupp Kfz. 70 trucks that the unit's official make up called for.

A nice profile view of a Krupp Protze L 2 H 43. Kfz. 69 towing a Pak 36/37 37 mm anti-tank gun seen during an exercise on Luneburger Heath in the summer of 1939. Note here the windshield side screens that are folded back whilst the windshield itself is folded down over the engine bonnet.

This anti-aircraft unit is seen driving through the suburbs of Rotterdam, Holland, in the summer of 1940. The unit appears to be equipped with 20 mm Flak 30s that are towed by Krupp Protze L 2 H 43. Kfz. 70s. Rotterdam was heavily bombed, famously hours after Holland had surrendered. Sadly that information was not transmitted to the German bomber force in time to turn back the raid.

Here a Krupp Protze L 2 H 43. Kfz. 69 is seen about to be used to tow another Krupp out of a small ditch that it has broken down near. Of note is the camouflaged poncho tied over the engine bonnet of the vehicle in the foreground and the soldier walking the tow rope back to the vehicle in need of assistance.

A nice overhead view of a selection of vehicles belonging to a motorized infantry regiment taken in the garage area of their barracks in Hamburg, Germany. Amongst the vehicles we can see here are thirteen Krupp Protze L 2 H 43. Kfz. 70's, thirteen Kfz. 70 Horch heavy off-road passenger cars, two motorcycle combinations and a Horch Kfz. 15 command car. It is not possible to see enough of the large truck on the left of the photo to enable identification of the truck type issued to this unit.

Opposite page, top: This is one of my favourite photos in my collection. It shows very clearly and in great detail a Krupp Kfz. 69 that has been improvised to mount its previously towed Pak 36/37 37 mm anti-tank gun on its back, to become a more useable anti-tank weapon in a fast moving war. The Kfz. 69 is being refuelled from a 200 litre fuel drum transported in the rear flat bed of a Einheits-Diesel off-road truck.

Opposite page, bottom:
Another great quality photograph of a motorized Anti-Tank unit that is equipped with a mix of Kfz. 69 trucks and BMW R12 motorcycle and sidecars, due to the lack of suitable motorized vehicles in the German Army's available motor pool.

A nice portrait photo of a 20 mm Flak 30 crew and their Krupp Protze L 2 H 43. Kfz. 70s. Of note in this photo is the protective anti-glare cover for both the windscreen and the side panels.

This small group of officers are seen having a discussion whilst standing next to a rather muddy Krupp Protze L 2 H 43 Kfz. 69 with its full wet weather tilt erected. Note the two-piece front bumper, shorter than the longer one-piece bumper on the L 2 H 243, one of the key recognition features of the latter type of Protze. The truck behind the Protze is a Büssing-NAG type 500. The photo was taken in southern Russia on 3rd October 1941.

An atmospheric photograph of a Krupp Protze L 2 H 43 Kfz. 70 driving through a gully as the bridge over it has been blown up. This photo was taken on 24th May 1940 during the 18 day-long battle for Belgium.

This picture, whilst looking similar to the one above, was actually taken in Yugoslavia in the spring of 1941. The Germans invaded Yugoslavia on 6th April 1941. The photo depicts a column of motorized infantry equipped with Krupp Protze L 2 H 43 Kfz. 70s. Note the Kfz. 70 in front of the column is towing a Sd.Ah. 32 small arms ammunition trailer.

Pictured here we see the rear of a Kfz. 69 that is towing the rarely photographed 75 mm *Leichtes Infanteriegeschutz* 18 (Light Infantry Howitzer) through the streets of Brussels, Belgium, in 1940. The structure in the background is one of the city's bus stops with a news stand advertising kiosk in front of it. This kiosk would usually have the front page of a newspaper on show or an advertising poster of some kind. These kiosks were common throughout European cities in the first part of the 20th century

This column of Krupp Kfz. 70s belonging to an anti-aircraft Gun unit equipped with 20 mm Flak 30s is seen driving through a Belgian suburb in the early summer of 1940. Of note is the stowage of the crew's rucksacks on the rear of the vehicle – an easy improvement to add to any model.

Here a Krupp Kfz. 70 belonging to a *Luftwaffe* anti-aircraft unit equipped with Flak 30s is seen during a training exercise. Note the three-tone camouflage scheme that adorns the Kfz70 – it is the earth-yellow, brown and green pre-war pattern.

Another column of Krupp Kfz. 70s, this time seen in north-eastern Holland in 1940. The vehicles are all towing the beautifully designed small 60 cm searchlight, mounted on their Sd.Anh. 51 transportation trailers.

15

This Krupp Kfz. 69, that is towing a 37 mm Pak 36/37 anti-tank gun, has been photographed having wheel chains fitted. The photo also gives us a good view of the vehicle's jack and other stowage on and around the front mudguard.

Belonging to the same flak unit, we have here an Sd.Kfz. 7 half-track towing a 88 mm Flak 18 being followed by an overloaded Krupp Kfz. 69 towing an ammunition trailer. Unfortunately it is impossible to identify the type of trailer as it is too obscured.

This study of a Krupp Kfz. 70 from a high angle gives us a great view of the typical crew stowage around this type of vehicle. Most evident here is the amount of food-related items that this crew have acquired. In sight we have milk churns, a large jar of preserves and a box full of assorted tins. The towed load is a covered 20 mm Flak 30.

A nice view of a Krupp Protze L 2 H 43 Kfz. 70 belonging to a *Luftwaffe* anti-aircraft unit equipped with 20 mm Flak 30. Of note here is the wet weather cover over the driver's compartment and two well-made log and wire fascines stowed behind the headlamps, one on each of the front mudguards.

This winter scene is typical of many across Russia in the early part of the war. The crew have set up a billet in a commandeered farm house. The Krupp Kfz. 70 parked up outside is fully covered with a full set of wet weather gear, including the rarely-seen cab door covers. Also of interest are the white painted width markings on the front mudguards and the white painted outer portions of the front bumper.

A *Luftwaffe* convoy pictured at the halt on a road in northern France. The lead vehicle is a saloon car, a Mercedes 170. The following vehicle is a Krupp Kfz. 70 that is towing a 60 cm searchlight. Of note is the raised weather tilt covering the whole vehicle from cab to the rear of the cargo bed. As was common amongst the German military the selection of vehicles in this convoy are a mix types and manufacturers. Standardization was to remain a goal throughout the war but was never even nearly achieved.)

An interesting configuration on this Krupp Protze L 2 H 43 Kfz. 70 that is parked outside a Russian town house in the autumn of 1942. The vehicle has its load bed fitted with its wet weather tilt and the driver's cab tilt is also mounted but has been folded back against the support rail for the leading edge of the load bed. The windshield is fitted with its anti-glare cover and folded down.

This nice quality photograph is of a Krupp Kfz. 70 about to be refuelled from a 200 litre fuel drum transported in the rear flat bed of an Einheits-Diesel off-road truck. Note on the Krupp's engine bonnet the brackets for a roll of barbed wire. This was a standard addition to the field engineers' units issued with the Krupp "Boxer".

Here we have an overall view of a Krupp Protze L 2 H 43 Kfz. 70 towing a 20 mm Flak 30 that is not fitted with its gun shield. It is in near parade ground condition with all is crew in full dress and not a piece of extra unauthorized stowage in sight. Not at all what was seen in actual battlefield service. A last clue as to this being a peacetime pre-war service photograph is the lack of covers over the headlights.

An infantry convoy on the road during the first days of the German invasion of Poland. Note the horse-drawn units at the bottom of the hill about to cross the bridge. The motorised section of the regiment is equipped with the Krupp-Protze Kfz. 70 and their protection from air attack is provided by Sd.Kfz. 10/4s, seen here towing their Sd.Anh. 51 trailers.

An oddball here as this is a pair *Luftwaffe* Krupp Kfz. 70 light trucks that are both painted in light grey, probably RLM 02. Also of interest is the pair of hand-held signal paddles in a bracket on the passenger side of the cargo bed sidewall panel.

This Krupp Kfz. 70 seen in Poland in the winter of 1940/41 is clearly marked as belonging to a motorized Anti-Tank unit, by the triangle on two small circles symbol painted in white on the driver's side front wing. Also of note is the barbed wire held in brackets stowed on top of the engine bonnet, and the NCO looking at a Michelin road map.

A high quality photo of a Krupp Kfz. 69 that is being used as the podium/dais for the Commanding Officer of this motorized Anti-Tank Gun unit that is equipped with the 37 mm Pak 36/37. The photo was taken on 7th June 1939 at the unit's barracks in Munster Germany. Note the three-tone pre-war camouflage scheme that uses earth-yellow, green and brown in thick wavy stripes all over the vehicle.

Another of my favourite photos from my collection is this image of a captured and repurposed Renault UE, seen here being used to tow its original fully tracked trailer. That in turn is coupled to a 37 mm Pak 36/37, this combination is just passing a parked up Krupp Kfz. 70 that itself is towing a 20 mm Flak 30.

This high quality photo shows a Krupp Protze L 2 H 43 Kfz. 69 parked in the Austrian town of St Polten on 14th March 1938, during the annexation of Austria that had begun on the 12th of the same month. Of note are the 20 litre jerry cans mounted in the rear and the tow rope wrapped around the tow hooks on the front of the chassis frame.

This parked up selection of vehicles represents the entire motor pool of a motorized infantry unit that is about to take part in a training exercise on Luneburger Heath in the summer of 1938. Note the large number of Krupp "Boxers" both at the far end of the front row as well as in the rows behind.

This anti-aircraft unit is seen in Greece in the summer of 1941. They are equipped with both Krupp Kfz. 70s and 20 mm Flak 38s. It is of note that, as has been seen, most of the anti-aircraft guns we have seen whilst in transit are covered with a canvas cover, not just keep them dry but also to keep the dust out of the breech mechanism. This was easily fouled and would cause a stoppage if not kept both lubricated and clean.

The column of vehicles we see here are taking part in an advance in central Russia in the late summer of 1941. It is a motorized anti-aircraft unit equipped with 20 mm Flak 30s towed by Krupp "Boxers". In this photo we also have a common vehicle but one rarely photographed, as it was purely utilitarian and not exciting in any way. It is an Opel Blitz 1.5 ton panel van often seen in the service of the German Post Office (*Deutsche Reichspost*) and even the German PK (Propaganda) Units.

This is a nice photo of a busy road junction somewhere in central Russia in the summer of 1941. The Krupp Kfz. 70 in the centre of the photo belongs to an anti-aircraft unit equipped with 20 mm anti-aircraft guns, the unit is part of General Heinz Wilhelm Guderian's Army Group North as denoted by the large letter "G" painted in white on the rear panel of the truck. There is also a unit badge but sadly I can't make it out for sure. Then on the upper driver's side rear of the panel there is painted in yellow a rendition of the German army infantry assault badge.

An interesting photo of a Krupp Kfz. 70 that has had a 20 mm Flak 30 mounted in its rear load area. Its equipment stowage is of interest as well, with 20 litre jerry cans tied on its side with rope. The truck is towing a supply of ammunition in an Sd.Anh. 51 trailer. The photo was taken in Yugoslavia in the spring of 1942.

Despite the relaxed atmosphere of this photo, that looks more like picnic than troops advancing in to France in 1940 as the Krupp Kfz. 69s are parked close together, the troops' rifles left in the motorcycle's side car, yet this was actually taken in early June 1940 whilst Dunkirk was still underway. The fight was still most definitely going on, but not evidently here.

A great view of the rear of a Krupp Kfz. 69. This angle is not often photographed and is full of useful information. Of interest here are the leather seat covers, the dented ammunition box containers and the rack with the spare wheel mount. Lastly note the roll of barbed wire stowed in the rear.

A Krupp Protze L 2 H 43 Kfz. 70 that has been thoroughly wrecked after running over an anti-tank mine set as part of the Dunkirk perimeter. This photo was taken just east of the French village of Rexpoede on 12th June 1940, and according to the text on the photo's reverse the explosion killed all but one of the crew.

A quality photo of a motorized anti-tank unit that is equipped with both Krupp Protze L 2 H 43 Kfz. 69s and 37 mm Pak 36/37s. The photograph was taken just after the unit had returned to their assembly area, following a parade on 20th September 1938 through the town of Bielefeld. Parades like this were encouraged by the Nazi government to try and form a bond between the civilian population and the armed forces.

Bottom: Here we have a photo of the practice for yet another parade, this one to be held in Koblenz in February 1939. This anti-tank unit is also equipped with both Krupp Protze L 2 H 43 Kfz. 69s and 37 mm Pak 36/37s. Of note are the individual numbers painted on the passenger side rear ammunition box bin in white, the foremost is numbered 16.

The crew of this *Luftwaffe* Krupp Protze L 2 H 43 Kfz. 70 are watching two of their number replace a damaged wheel and also prepare the vehicle to be towed off the obstacle that it has become trapped on.

A good close up of a Krupp Protze L 2 H 43 Kfz. 70 photographed in Holland in the summer of 1940. If this date is correct, it is fascinating that the vehicle retains its pre-war three-colour camouflage. Of note in this photo is the canvas windshield cover over the folded down windshield, and the command pennant fitted that denotes the vehicle as belonging to this unit's command motor pool. Lastly we get a good look at the triangular oil can mounted above the spare wheel.

This photo was taken on the 18th of May 1940 whilst the Germans were on their march to the channel coast; the photo shows the driver/mechanic caring out the daily checks to ensure the continued running of the Krupp Protze L 2 H 43 Kfz. 70, of note other than the good engine compartment detail is the engines data plate fixed to the underside of the bonnet.

A rather motley looking *Luftwaffe* crew pose beside their Krupp Kfz. 70 that has been converted into a mobile flak vehicle by the addition of a 20 mm Flak 30 mounted in its rear load-carrying bed. The gun its self was mounted on a framework that raised its height in the vehicle, so that the barrel was not obstructed in its 360° turning ability by the truck's sides. The truck is towing the standard 20 mm ammunition trailer, the Sd.Anh. 51, but this one has had a rack mounted on its lid to enable it to be used to haul much of the crew's personal kit that had to be relocated to allow room in the truck itself for the gun mount.

This pair of *Luftwaffe* Krupp Kfz. 70s is seen in the summer of 1943 in northern France. It was common practice for an airfield to be protected by both fixed and mobile anti-aircraft guns. The mobile units would move on a regular basis so that the Allies could not pin-point all the flak sites around an airfield before any planned air raid.

A pair of *Luftwaffe* Krupp Kfz. 70s seen in the suburbs of Vilnius, Lithuania, during the German advance in the east of 1941. The local children are curious to take a look at who they originally thought were their liberators from Soviet oppression, but sadly the Germans soon proved to be as bad or worse. As the front-line troops moved off they were followed up by the murderous death squads of the *Einsatzgruppen*.

Here we see a Krupp Protze L 2 H 43 Kfz. 69 with an MG 34 mounted and a windshield cover over its windscreen, a roll of barbed wire mounted over its bonnet and 2 fascines one stowed above each front wing/fender. The crew look totally relaxed on the summer afternoon in the French countryside in the weeks after the French surrender and before new orders come to relocate before the next campaign that was to be in much colder climes.

This beautiful study of a *Luftwaffe* Krupp Kfz. 70 with an on-board mounted 20 mm Flak 30 was take in the midst of the huge plains of central Russia in the summer of 1942. The crew here are seen taking a break, one smoking his pipe and at least two others eating a snack.

A posed photograph, albeit very amateurish, it is typical of the type of photo taken to send home. Here we see two members of the crew posing with their Kar 98 rifles, next to their Krupp Kfz. 70 that is marked as belonging to a motorized anti-tank gun unit by the symbol on its driver's side mudguard. Note that the windshield has its canvas protective cover fitted but is still raised – this indicates the truck is parked for the night, as it is impossible to drive off and see where you are going with the cover fitted to the raised windscreen.

Seen crossing a river in Estonia in 1941, this *Luftwaffe* Krupp Kfz. 70 and its towed 20 mm Flak 30 are making good progress. Note the steam rising from the hot engine block and what looks to be a loudspeaker horn stowed on the side of the load bed, low down close to the wheel well.

Parked outside a German farm house the crew of this Krupp Kfz. 70, who have been billeted there during an exercise in the summer of 1938, are posing with the family who had hosted them. This was a common practice during an extended exercise that sometimes lasted up to four weeks.

This photo shows an impromptu orders group gathering during a halt in the advance into Russia. The photo is of great interest as it illustrates the huge variety of vehicles that a single unit had in their motor pool, that caused a logistics nightmare for the German army. We see in the lead a Krupp Kfz. 70 with a captured and repurposed ex-British army Bedford truck and a horse drawn supply wagon to the left, whilst behind the Krupp we can see another selection of vehicles that include a Horch staff car and at least one Hansa-Lloyd light truck.

Another atmospheric photo. In this one we see a *Luftwaffe* Krupp Kfz. 70 about to pass the twisted remains of a steel reinforced concrete bridge that has been destroyed completely. It is highly unusual for the number plate to be in reversed colours – white writing on a black background.

This is the business end of a Krupp Protze L 2 H 143 Kfz. 19 *Funkkraftwagen* (Radio Communications Vehicle). They were built on both the early and late types of Boxer chassis. The truck had a fully enclosed wooden van-style body that was fitted with a telescopic aerial that was 9 metres tall when raised. The aerial can be seen clearly mounted to the rear wall of the enclosed wooden body in this photo, along with the truck's five man *Luftwaffe* crew.

This unit "HQ" group has set up in a Russian farmyard for the night and troops of all ranks can be seen going about their tasks. The early type of Krupp Protze L 2 H 43 Kfz. 19 *Funkkraftwagen* (Radio Communications Vehicle) can be clearly recognized by its "Maratze" steel frame antenna mounted on its roof. Also worthy of note here is the odd stowage location of the fascine on the front wall of the wooden box body, above the driver's position.

Bottom: In this fine portrait we see the crew eating their dinner standing alongside their Krupp Protze L 2 H 43 Kfz. 19 *Fernsprechbetriebs-kraftwagen* (Field Telephone exchange van). Not a common vehicle as it was really too small for its assigned task and was replaced by production versions built on off-road trucks such as the Henschel D33, etc.

Krupp Protze L 2 H 143

This excellent quality photograph of the later type of a Krupp Protze L 2 H 143 Kfz. 69 illustrates well the key easily recognizable features that can be used to differentiate between this late version and the earlier type. The longer one piece front bumper and the larger gap between the pair of rear wheels are the easiest to spot. The picture was taken somewhere on a road between Lille and the French coast in June 1940. More of this vehicle will be seen later.

Another good quality photo of a Krupp Protze L 2 H 143 Kfz. 69. This one is seen in as-new condition and is parked in the marshalling yard of the Munster railway station, ready to be sent to its forward assembly area prior to Germany's invasion of the Low Countries in May 1940. It will not take long until the vehicle is adorned with all the little extras that a crew found useful and stowed in or on the vehicle, in any position they could find to attach it.

Opposite page bottom: Pictured here is a Krupp Protze L 2 H 143 Kfz. 70 that is just about to unhitch its towed 20 mm Flak 30. This photo taken in the northern battle sector of the Russian front in the early winter of 1941. The 20 mm Flak was also a very useful as a supplement to a ground units' fire power. Whilst this tree-line position would not be good for anti-aircraft defence it was very good concealment for a 20 mm weapon with ammo that was very effective against trucks and all types of Russian armoured cars of the time.

A pair of Krupp Protze L 2 H 143 Kfz. 69s is parked outside Bochum railway station. Note here the arched bar that is fixed to the top of the windshield – it was used to fix the leading edge of the canvas all-weather tilt in position.

This Krupp Protze L 2 H 143 Kfz. 70 has been driven off the road by an overly tired driver; this was a not uncommon accident all sides. This Krupp is about to be recovered, evidently it needed a new front tyre and a steering rod replaced before it got underway again. Of note here is the very rarely seen canvas back door – these were rarely used and often lost altogether.

Pictured driving though the Russian village of Polyanovo, approximately 130 km south-west of Moscow, this column of Krupp Protze L 2 H 143 Kfz. 70s belonging to a motorized anti-tank unit have halted and are preparing to spend the night. They will either commandeer a house or occupy an abandoned one, either are better than a night under canvas in the Russian winter.

This Krupp Protze L 2 H 143 Kfz. 69 has stopped for a group photo in the town of Gerersdorf. Even the German troops were mostly surprised by how welcome the Austrian public made them once they got out of the border areas where most of the naturalized Germans lived. This truck in as-new condition and as can be easily seen it has done no fighting or off-roading, but has made its way on the highways of rural Austria in the spring of 1938 without incident. Such was the *Anschluss*, the annexation of Austria into the greater German Reich.

This is a great study of a Krupp Protze L 2 H 143 Kfz. 69 that belongs to the 3rd Battery of a motorized anti-tank gun unit. Of note are the missing cap that should be covering the engine's staring dog, that can now be seen protruding from the vehicles louvered nose panel, the covered folded-down windshield and the roll of barbed wire stowed in custom brackets on the engine cover panel.

An anti-tank gun unit equipped with both Krupp Protze L 2 H 143 Kfz. 69 and 37 mm Pak 36/37 weapons is photographed dismounting their vehicles in order to set them up in a firing position. This is taking place on the training grounds attached to the barracks in Frankfurt, Germany, in the summer of 1938. Note that the troops are wearing caps and uniforms which were not typical of the *Wehrmacht* at this time.

This German column is seen driving through a typical village in Latvia during the advance in the summer of 1941. It is being led by a Krupp Protze L 2 H 143 Kfz. 70 marked as belonging to General Guderian's Army Group North, as denoted by the large letter "G" painted in white on the passenger's side wing. The "G" was usually painted on the driver's side but it is by no means unique to find it on the passenger's side.

Here is a quality photo of a Krupp Protze L 2 H 143 Kfz. 70 driving at speed through rural France in the summer of 1942. Of note in this picture is the map case hanging on the rear centre of the back wall of the driver's cab, the folded-down covered windshield and the bent front bumper. There is a feeble attempt at camouflage by adding foliage at the front and rear.

This iconic view must have been photographed thousands of times by the victorious German soldiers as they strutted around Paris after the French surrender. This is the Place de Concorde in central Paris, the truck is an Krupp Protze L 2 H 143 Kfz. 69. Of note are the two Kar 98 rifles stowed in the driver's cab in brackets mounted on the firewall panel. As an aside there were originally two Egyptian obelisks in the Place de Concorde but following the defeat of Napoleon one hundred and forty years earlier the British took one as a war prize and it is now located on the north bank of the river Thames in central London.

A heavily loaded Krupp Protze L 2 H 143 Kfz. 69, loaded to the extent that the gun crew must ride standing on the running boards and holding onto the canvas tilt support bars. Of note here are the Kar 98s in their racks but wrapped up in a canvas roll and the extra stowage on top of the barbed wire roll on the bonnet. I am not sure what the small wheel on the back is for but it certainly is not standard equipment.

On a road somewhere in Yugoslavia in 1942, we have here a column of Krupp Protze L 2 H 143 Kfz. 70s. Note the fascine tied onto the passenger's side wing and also the MG 34 mounted in the rear bed on the wall immediately behind the driver's bench seat.

Seen on one of the many trips a unit would make around its barrack area we have here the crew of a Krupp "Boxer" posing with a local girl for a photo. The German armed forces under the National Socialists realized early on that it was good politics for them to foster an empathy between the civilian population and the military, to encourage the feeling of one Germany acting together i.e. the people's army. Prior to this the army was not viewed as anything more than an instrument of the state.

With a 20 mm Flak 38 mounted in the modified rear cargo bed this Krupp Protze L 2 H 143 Kfz. 70 towing a Sd.Anh. 51 ammunition trailer looks every inch to be fit for purpose. However in fact, whilst the advantage of the gun being mounted in the back was speed into action, the lack of a large enough gun platform made reloading an issue from most angles.

This parade in Prague in 1942 must have been one of the most photographed events in that year. I have seen many photos of it from official sources but this one was taken by a soldier who was there at the time. It shows a nice rear view of a Krupp Protze L 2 H 143 Kfz. 69 towing a 75 mm *leichtes Infanteriegeschütz 18*.

We see here on a bright and sunny spring day in northern Austria an Einheits-Diesel towing a Krupp Protze L 2 H 143 Kfz. 69 artillery tractor variant. Unfortunately I have no other information on this photo, but it appears to have been taken in 1939 or 1940, as the camouflage on the Krupp is still the three-tone pre-war colour scheme, yet the truck is in overall panzer grey.

Whilst it is common to see allied trucks in service with the German armed forces, it is decidedly uncommon to see a German vehicle in wartime service with the Allies. Here we have a Krupp Protze L 2 H 143 Kfz. 70 in service with an Allied unit in southern Italy in 1944. The helmets are ex-British, but the uniforms are clearly not, and unfortunately I have no more information on this interesting photo.

Bottom: Photographed during a parade through the town of Duisburg, Germany, in 1938 we see here a *Luftwaffe* anti-aircraft unit equipped with both the Krupp Protze L 2 H 143 Kfz. 70 and a 20 mm Flak 30. Note that unusually there is no gun shield fitted to the Flak 30.

A nice snapshot of the rear of a pair of Protze L 2 H 143 Kfz. 69s. They are parked up under the shade of a tree on a hot summer's day in northern France during the summer of 1943. If I am able to assume that this photo was taken close to others in the same album, it was taken somewhere on the Cherbourg peninsula in northern France.

This view of a Krupp Protze L 2 H 143 Kfz. 69 shows a truck on a French road in October 1940. Of interest here is the collection of markings on the driver's side wing, we have the white triangle of an anti-tank gun unit, the white number 3 to its side denoting it belongs to the 3rd company and lastly the 36th Infanterie Division symbol is painted in yellow just below the Notek Light. Note that yellow looks dark on this type of black and white film.

This *Luftwaffe* crew pose standing next to their Protze L 2 H 143 Kfz. 70 in the first snows of winter 1939. The photo was taken in the grounds of a park in Potsdam, 25 km south-west of Berlin. Of note is the pristine nature of this new vehicle, especially the canvas wet weather tilt as they seem to age very quickly once in service. Lastly note the fitting of the driver's hand operated spotlight slung under the mounting arm for the vehicles "trafficator", the indicator arm that popped out 90° to indicate an imminent turn.

This interesting photo was taken by the driver of the first Krupp Kfz. 70 in the line. The camera he is using belongs to the *Luftwaffe* lance-corporal standing next to the soldier sitting in the driver's seat of the first vehicle; note the empty camera case hanging from the *gefreiter*'s neck. Note the pre-war style gasmask in a canvas satchel.

This Protze L 2 H 143 Kfz. 70 is photographed on 9th September 1942 in the woods just east of the airfield based close to the French coastal town of Le-Touquet. The officer standing next to the truck is holding a signalling paddle, the truck itself is towing an *Sonderanhänger* (*1 achs.*) (Sd.Ah. 51) trailer and the barrel of the flak gun is visible in the photo. The same "U" shaped trailer base unit was used to transport the gun or an ammunition box, as well as the 60 cm searchlight.

This column of Krupp Protze L 2 H 143 Kfz. 70s that belong to a motorized infantry regiment are seen taking part in the first stage of the Austrian *Anschluss*. The German army were welcomed by crowds of the naturalized Germans who lived in the border areas, they lined the roads in villages and towns and often showered the army with bottles of wine, flowers and other gifts of welcome. These trucks are festooned with flowers but they still have their MG 34 machine guns fixed to the vehicle at the ready.

The scene at the docks at the port of Boulogne sur Mer in northern France. Boulogne was far less damaged than the ports of Calais and Dunkirk a few miles down the coast and was just one of the many assembly points for abandoned and damaged vehicles retrieved from the local battlefields. In this picture we can see two British QF 3.7-inch anti-aircraft guns, one 40 mm Bofors anti-aircraft gun and in the centre a damaged Krupp Protze L 2 H 143 Kfz. 70 that has many tyres missing, as well as its spare wheel on the driver's side.

Seen here in Normandy France in the autumn of 1942 close to the town of Flers we find a troop of *Luftwaffe* Krupp Protze L 2 H 143 Kfz. 70 towing their 20 mm Flak 30's. Other than the relaxed looking crew members of note is the roll of chicken wire wedged between the flak gun and the trailers mudguard. As a note to diorama builders out there the narrow gauge railway track that can be seen next to the road was and still is a common sight running along many of the roadsides of the inland areas of Normandy, France.

Another of the few photographs from my collection that were taken in the occupied British Channel Islands, the only part of Britain to be under German occupation during the war. This photo was taken on Jersey on 3rd October 1941 and is a study of one of the few German vehicles to be transported to the island, a Krupp Protze L 2 H 143 Kfz. 70. Note the MG 34 fitted to the vehicle and the unusual stowage position of a roll of barbed wire against the side wall in the rear load bed.

A nice photo of a motorized rifle company on the move through the border area between Belgium and France on the road towards Sedan. The symbol for the rifle company is painted in white on the driver's side front wing, it is a rectangle on top of two small circles.

A *Luftwaffe* Krupp Protze L 2 H 143 Kfz. 70 towing a well wrapped up 20 mm Flak 30. There is some interesting stowage on this truck – the rear cargo bed panel has a 20 litre jerry can tied to it and on the side wall a set of pioneer tools are mounted in brackets. Then an unrolled fascine has been tied to the stowed unditching board, the part rolled back tilt is of note as well.

Parked up on the border between Poland and Belarus these Krupp Protze L 2 H 143 Kfz. 70s in their Panzer Grey paint job stand out starkly against the snow-covered countryside. Of note are the snow chains fitted to the rearmost wheels and the clean uncluttered appearance of these vehicles. This makes me think that they are replacement vehicles being driven forward from a rail head close by.

A motorized anti-tank gun unit on the march through a suburb of Arras, France, a French town that suffered bombardment in both world wars. Note that the unit is equipped with both the Krupp Protze L 2 H 143 Kfz. 70 and the earlier L 2 H 43 Kfz. model, and that the front two Krupps both have barbed wire stowed in custom brackets on the engine cover panel whilst the following trucks don't.

This Krupp Protze L 2 H 143 Kfz. 69 has slipped in to a ditch and is under the process of being recovered; of note are the two unditching boards and the damaged suspension clearly visible from this view.

This Krupp Protze L 2 H 143 Kfz. 70 that belongs to a motorized anti-tank unit is seen here parked outside a Russian barn in the summer of 1941 in the early stages of Operation Barbarossa. Of note in this photo are the barbed wire mounted on the bonnet and the tow rope wrapped around the tow hook on the front of the chassis, the windshield without side panels in its protective cover and lastly the mix of uniform and civilian clothing worn by the crew. This is either the 87th or 134th Infanterie Division, both used the heart insignia.

A very muddy Krupp Protze L 2 H 143 Kfz. 70 is making its way across the Russian steppe in the late summer of 1941. Note the rarely seen full set of canvas wet weather covers are fitted, including the doors on both the driver's cab and the tail gate, also the lack of field tools as they are missing from their custom stowage locations. Even the tyre has gone from the spare wheel.

Seen here is a Krupp Protze L 2 H 143 Kfz. 70 that has become stuck in the soft ground on the training grounds close to the barracks in Paderborn, Germany. We can see two main group of troops, one pushing the truck from the rear and another pulling on a rope attached to the front attempting to free the vehicle. The officers however wander about – doing something important I am sure.

A nice study of a Krupp Protze L 2 H 143 Kfz. 69 seen driving around a field in the Frankfurt area. The driver is one Private Adolf Michener and he was undergoing driver training. The photograph was taken on 7th June 1939.

This is a Krupp Protze L 2 H 143 Kfz. 69 towing its 37 mm Pak 36/37, seen on 8th June 1940 in Northern France. Having left the Dunkirk perimeter this motorized Anti-Tank Gun unit is now part of the force chasing the British rearguard south-west along the French coast. The poncho over the bonnet is a good addition to the vehicle's camouflage and the MG 34 on its mount is of interest, but what I find most interesting is the variation on the tactical symbol on the driver's side fender. It is missing one of the small circles (wheels) under the triangle. Lastly the tennis racket wedged in between the driver's hand operated spotlight and the body of the cab is an odd addition.

This is the same Krupp Protze L 2 H 143 Kfz. 69 as seen on the previous page but earlier on in the campaign. This photo was taken on 21st May 1940. The anti-tank unit has already come across French armour, as witnessed by the French tank crew helmet slung over the driver's side headlight. In this view we get an excellent look at the unfinished tactical badge with its one wheel and the rubber bulb operated horn mounted on the cab. Certainly not standard, but a whimsical crew addition like the tennis racket that appeared later.

Dinner time for the crew. This Krupp Protze L 2 H 143 Kfz. 69 is parked next to a French house on the D939, just north-west of the village of Marquion. It was very common for advertisements to be painted on roadside houses in France, it still happens today but not as much. Note the Kar 98 rifle lent up against the front bumper and the empty rack (an oval hoop on the footplate of the cab and a toggle-clasp mounted on the cab door post on the same level as the bottom of the instrument panel dash-board).

Another photograph of a Krupp Protze L 2 H 143 Kfz. 70 driving through the town of Arras, France. This time, however, it is after the fighting has moved on. This photo was taken on 2nd June 1940 whilst the battle of Dunkirk, only a few miles north-west, was still in full swing. Note the cloth tied over the engine bonnet with a large white swastika sewn onto it. It is not a German flag as it has no white circle.

A *Luftwaffe* NCO looks back over his charges, a convoy of Krupp Protze L 2 H 143 Kfz. 70s towing 20 mm Flak 30s. Note the flak gun has no shield and is covered by a tarpaulin of some kind, also again note the windshield cover. This photo was taken in May 1942 somewhere close to the barracks at Koblenz, Germany.

This Krupp Protze L 2 H 143 Kfz. 69, still attached to its 37 mm anti-tank gun, has been rolled over during a night drive. Sadly the crew did not make it, all six men died. The accident happened on the night of the 4/5th August 1942 on a road close to the town of Hengelo, Holland.

An excellent profile of one of the rare Krupp Protze L 2 H 143 Kfz. 19's seen parked up in the back streets of Mostar, Yugoslavia during the advance south towards Greece. Both the timber board construction of the body work and the steel frame "Maratze" radio antenna are very prominent in this view.

Krupp Protze L 2 H 143 Kfz. 19 *Funkkraftwagen* (Radio Communications Vehicle) – we can see the top of the collapsed telescopic aerial that is covered by a canvas sheath protruding from the driver's side at the back of the truck. I can only identify two of the following three trucks, the one behind the Krupp Kfz. 68 is a Mercedes 3 ton and the one at the very back is a Phanomen Granit 1500.

Loaded on a flatbed railway car is a Krupp Protze L 2 H 143 Kfz. 19 *Fernsprechbetriebskraftwagen mit Fahrgestell* (Field Telephone Exchange Van). Of note is that all the external stowage has been removed before the journey.

This is one of the very rare Krupp Protze L 2 H 143 Kfz. 68 *Funkmastkraftwagen* (Radio Aerial Mast Vehicles). It can be recognised by the folded down telescopic aerial mast that is laid flat on the centre line of the truck's roof, and even overhangs the windshield. The truck behind the Krupp Kfz. 68 is an Einheits Diesel *Funkmastkraftwagen* Kfz. 68 and the truck behind that is a Krupp L 3 H 163 Kfz. 72 radio truck, as are the next two in line. This radio communications unit is making its way to the forward assembly area for the imminent invasion of the Low Countries in May 1940.

Parked in a river getting a quick wash is a Krupp Protze L 2 H 43 Kfz. 19 *Funkkraftwagen* (Radio Communications Vehicle). It can be clearly recognized by its "Maratze" steel frame antenna mounted on the roof. Upon closer inspection it might be that the crew are just playing in the river, as it looks like the water is missing the truck and is on its way towards the other crew man just visible on the far side of the truck.

Posing next to the Krupp Protze L 2 H 143 Kfz. 69 that they are working on is a pair of mechanics. The vehicle belongs to a motorized anti-tank gun unit as denoted by the tactical marking on the driver's side front wing. The Krupps seen here both have a bracket attached to the centre on the bumper – this is the front part of the bracket to hold a roll of barbed wire, as shown on page 20 for example.

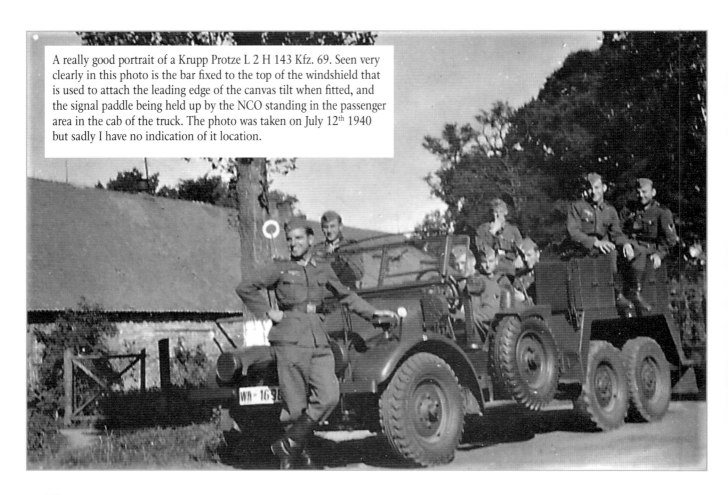

A really good portrait of a Krupp Protze L 2 H 143 Kfz. 69. Seen very clearly in this photo is the bar fixed to the top of the windshield that is used to attach the leading edge of the canvas tilt when fitted, and the signal paddle being held up by the NCO standing in the passenger area in the cab of the truck. The photo was taken on July 12th 1940 but sadly I have no indication of it location.

A nice close-up portrait of the driver's cab area of a Krupp Protze L 2 H 143 Kfz. 70. Of note is the cover over the driver's hand operated spotlight seen in the foreground, the stowed oil can over the spare wheel and the manufacturer's detail plate fitted to the front of the side panel of the cargo bed.

This view of another Krupp Protze L 2 H 143 Kfz. 70 gives us a close-up of the drivers cab area from the other side note on this truck the helmets and mess tin stowed on the hooks for the wet weather tilt, the *Luftwaffe* crew man looks to be seated comfortably but I can assure you that a drive over anything but smooth terrain in one of these vehicles is not at all relaxing.

A great picture with a Krupp Protze L 2 H 143 Kfz. 69 prominent in the view, of note is the stowage piled up on the bonnet and the barbed wire; it looks to include a 20 litre jerry can and a log fascine. The Krupp is towing a 37 mm Pak 36/37 anti-tank gun. The large covered lorry in the back ground is a Büssing-NAG type 4500 A.

Another view of a Krupp Protze L 2 H 143 Kfz. 70, this one belongs to the *Luftwaffe*, and is seen negotiating a very steep hill. To ensure the vehicle does not slip all the crew have got out to walk down, even the NCO in the passenger seat is sitting to one side so he can get out quickly should the need arise.

A photo of the same vehicle that was photographed having is engine worked on previously in this publication. Here we see it negotiating a cross country course on a training ground. The front retainer for the roll of barbed wire is visible, as are the two other retainers near to the windscreen.

This impromptu photograph was taken of a line-up of an anti-tank platoon's Krupp Protze L 2 H 143 Kfz. 69s. It was taken on 9th May 1940, the day before this unit became part of the invading forces that crossed the Dutch border as part of the first actions of the war in the west. The motorcycle and sidecar in this view is a BMW R-750.

This Krupp Protze L 2 H 143 Kfz. 70 photo is very useful, as it actually shows a trafficator in operation. Whilst the older readers amongst you may remember these devices on cars, most now will never have seen them and the many photographs of the retaining housing on many wartime vehicles does nothing to explain their use. In this photo the indicator arm of the passenger's side trafficator is extended, indicating that a right turn is being executed.

Seen here a photo taken whilst a motorized unit is preparing for an upcoming unit inspection. The photo was taken on 10th July 1939 at this unit's barracks in the Potsdam area, a suburb of Berlin, Germany.

This is a platoon of a motorized rifle company, note the tactical symbol painted on the driver's side wings/fenders. The unit is seen leaving the scene of their latest attack, a Ukrainian hamlet that they have put to the torch and now leave burning in their wake. This scene was repeated many hundreds of times during the merciless invasion of the east.

A nice close-up portrait view of a Krupp Protze L 2 H 143 Kfz. 69 and it crew as well as other soldiers on a jetty constructed over a river bank by military engineers during an exercise. They are all awaiting on the return of the ferry to cross the river. Whilst not in this view, the ferry was made from four German bridging pontoons. The troops wear WW1 style helmets, and the umpire has a white band around his cap. Lastly of note is the tactical symbol for a motorized anti-tank unit unusually painted on the side of the vehicle as well as on the usual place at the rear.

This is a very poor quality photo of a Krupp Protze L 2 H 143 Kfz. 70 with a 20 mm Flak 30 mounted in the rear cargo bed, the photo has been badly damaged by both sun light and damp, but it still remains a fascinating photograph of a crew posing for an unofficial crew portrait, the shot was taken in July 1943 in the Pas-de-Calais, France. I strongly recommend that you take time to look at all the detail in this photo and also just in case you are wondering the weapon the crew member is resting on the tail gate is a Bergman MP 34 sub-machine gun. This Krupp belonged to a *Luftwaffe* airfield protection unit.

This photo is of a complete troop of the very rare Krupp Protze L 2 H 143 Kfz. 83 *Leichter Scheinwerferkraftwagen I.* (60 cm Searchlight Prime Mover Type 1). It was a standard Kfz. 70 variant fitted out with an 8 kw electrical generator to power the searchlight in the rear of the truck bed. The Type 2 vehicles did not have the generator in the rear of the vehicle.

This Krupp Protze L 2 H 143 Kfz. 69 has had its rear end ammunition stowage altered in order to provide more room for the gun crew needed to man this improvised tank killer. The 37 mm Pak 36/37 is mounted just behind the driver's cab, right in the front of the load bed, and an armoured front end to the vehicle has been manufactured from steel plates welded together. They have been mounted sloped with no vertical shot traps, however the vision for the driver is much impaired as the small vision hatch is some distance from the driving position.

This photo is of the same improvised tank killer as seen above. Note here the re-designed gun shield and also the addition of two Notek lights fixed to the sloped armour over the engine compartment. The armoured door to the starter dog is left open and is hanging down. In my humble opinion the advantages this conversion offered were probably more than outweighed by the difficulties it brought to the normal operation of the vehicle, through restriction to the driver's forward vision and the overloading of both the front suspension and also the steering system.

Sd.Kfz. 247 Ausf A

This Sd.Kfz. 247 Ausf A is being used by a high ranking officer to conduct a review of units under his command. Note the other two officers in the Sd.Kfz. 247, one in a standard *Wehrmacht* uniform, the other in the all black Panzer soldier's uniform, and the actual troops stood to attention from both units.

This Sd.Kfz. 247 Ausf A is seen amidst an orders group. The vehicle was built on the "Boxer" chassis and whilst looking at first sight a good vehicle, it was in fact woefully under-powered and the armour too thin to be of much use. As such production of the type did not last long and was soon superseded by the Sd.Kfz. 247 Ausf B, based on a modified Horch heavy off-road passenger car chassis.

This panzer division's reconnaissance unit is seen in Brunswick, Germany, on a sunny day in April 1940. The lead vehicle is an Sd.Kfz. 247 Ausf A in overall Panzer Grey. Of interest is the lack of headlight covers on any of the visible vehicles, which indicates that the unit is not expecting to go into combat any time soon.

This photo is of an Sd.Kfz. 247 Ausf A about to take part in a parade in Vienna, Austria, to celebrate the annexation of Austria into the Greater German Reich in 1938. Note the surreal mix of flowers and a roll of barbed wire on the engine cover plate.

This armoured reconnaissance unit is preparing for a parade through Berlin to celebrate Hitler's birthday on 20th April 1938. Amongst the vehicles seen accompanying this Sd.Kfz. 247 Ausf A are Sd.Kfz. 223 4-wheeled radio cars and some 6-wheeled Sd.Kfz. 231s.